DATE DUE _____

DEMCO

Zigzag Movement

by Lola M. Schaefer

Consulting Editor: Gail Saunders-Smith, Ph.D.

Consultant: P. W. Hammer, Ph.D., Acting Manager
of Education, American Institute of Physics

Pebble Books

an imprint of Capstone Press
Mankato, Minnesota

Pebble Books are published by Capstone Press
818 North Willow Street, Mankato, Minnesota 56001
http://www.capstone-press.com

Library of Congress Cataloging-in-Publication Data
Schaefer, Lola M., 1950–
    Zigzag movement/by Lola M. Schaefer.
    p. cm.—(The way things move)
    Includes bibliographical references and index.
    Summary: Simple text and photographs show people and things that make
zigzag movements.
    ISBN 0-7368-0401-3
    1. Motion—Juvenile literature. [1. Motion.] I. Title. II. Series.
QC133.5.S34   2000
531′.3—dc21   99-18413
                                                                CIP

Note to Parents and Teachers

The series The Way Things Move supports national science standards for units on understanding motion and the principles that explain it. The series also shows that things move in many different ways. This book describes and illustrates zigzag movement. The photographs support early readers in understanding the text. The repetition of words and phrases helps early readers learn new words. This book also introduces early readers to subject-specific vocabulary words, which are defined in the Words to Know section. Early readers may need assistance to read some words and to use the Table of Contents, Words to Know, Read More, Internet Sites, and Index/Word List sections of the book.

Table of Contents

Zigzag movement is motion from side to side.

Zigzag movement makes a sharp turn at each side.

A zigzag looks like this.

Sewing machine needles zigzag.

Sailboats zigzag
across water.

Hands zigzag to write.

Players zigzag checkers across a board.

Skiers zigzag down hills.

Soccer players zigzag down a field.

Words to Know

movement—the act of changing position from place to place

sailboat—a boat that moves through the water by wind blowing against its sails; sailboats use the wind to zigzag across a body of water; this action is called tacking.

sewing machine—a machine used for sewing very fast or making special stitches; sewing machines can make zigzag stitches.

sharp—at a small angle; a zigzag motion has a sharp turn from side to side.

skier—a person who travels down snow-covered hills or mountains on skis; skiers zigzag to slow their speed and control their movements.

soccer—a game in which players score by kicking a ball into a goal at each end of a field; the way players pass a ball down a field makes a zigzag.

Read More

Canizares, Susan and Betsey Chessen. *Make It Move!* Science Emergent Readers. New York: Scholastic, 1999.

Challoner, Jack. *The Visual Dictionary of Physics.* Eyewitness Visual Dictionaries. New York: Dorling Kindersley, 1995.

Pinna, Simon de. *Forces and Motion.* Science Projects. Austin, Texas: Raintree Steck-Vaughn, 1998.

Internet Sites

Home Demos of Science
http://nyelabs.kcts.org/homedemos/index.html

Physics4Kids: Motion
http://www.kapili.com/physics4kids/motion/index.html

Index/Word List

across, 13, 17
checkers, 17
down, 19, 21
hands, 15
hills, 19
looks, 9
machine, 11
motion, 5
movement, 5, 7
needles, 11
players, 17, 21

sailboats, 13
sewing, 11
sharp, 7
side, 5, 7
skiers, 19
soccer, 21
turn, 7
water, 13
write, 15
zigzag, 5, 7, 9, 11,
  13, 15, 17, 19, 21

Word Count: 50
Early-Intervention Level: 8

Editorial Credits

Martha E. H. Rustad, editor; Timothy Halldin, cover designer; Heidi Schoof,
  photo researcher

Photo Credits

David F. Clobes, 14
Index Stock, 16
International Stock/Kirk Anderson, cover
James P. Rowan, 12
Kate Boykin, 10
Unicorn Stock Photos/Dede Gilman, 1; B. W. Hoffman, 6; Maren Holsinger
  Mullen, 8; Aneal Vohra, 20
Uniphoto, 4
Visuals Unlimited/Hugh Rose, 18